Also by Judith Mattison

Beginnings: For the Newly Married

Who Will Listen to Me?: Prayer Thoughts for
   High School Girls

Life Is Good, Life Is Hard

DIVORCE
—The Pain & The Healing

DIVORCE
—The Pain & The Healing

Personal Meditations
When Marriage Ends

Judith Mattison

AUGSBURG Publishing House • Minneapolis

DIVORCE—THE PAIN AND THE HEALING
Personal Meditations When Marriage Ends

Photos: Hildegard Adler, 18; Jean-Claude Lejeune, 24, 29, 50, 79, 86; Bob Combs, 39, 43; Dave Swan, 66; Wallowitch, 94.

Library of Congress Cataloging in Publication Data

Mattison, Judith M.
  DIVORCE—THE PAIN AND THE HEALING.

  1. Divorce—Religious aspects—Christianity—
Meditations.   I. Title.
BT707.M37   1985   261.8'3589   85-11140
ISBN 0-8066-2128-1

Manufactured in the U.S.A.   APH 10-1905

    3   4   5   6   7   8   9   0   1   2   3   4   5   6   7   8   9

*This book is dedicated to
Tom and Diane Brady,
who opened their home
and their hearts to me
during my days of transition.*

Contents

Preface: The Emotions of Divorce

Divorce is an inevitably painful experience, regardless of the circumstances. I have felt it was also so individual, so unique in each couple's history and experience that it wasn't possible to write about it.

It was the urging of friends and people whom I've come to know in small groups which met to discuss divorce which has led me to write this book. I've discovered, through their candid sharing, that there are universal feelings which divorced and separated persons share, regardless of individual backgrounds. Seeing those emotions expressed on paper may help us travel the difficult and sometimes lonely path from separation to new wholeness.

This book is also for married and single people as they attempt to understand and be sensitive to divorced people they know and love.

Finally, this is a book of healing. I believe wounds heal more rapidly when the true depth of their pain is confronted and spoken. Spiritually, we draw close to God's presence as we recognize and openly acknowledge our weaknesses as well as when we turn for help and finally, as a healed person, in gratitude to God.

Divorce gives us opportunity for self-examination, compassion, sharing in community and renewal. It is, in that way, an opportunity for Christian growth.

Tension

No matter what I'd been doing,
it was always when I began
to drive back home
that my jaw clenched
tight.
I carried the weight of our relationship
clutched in my head,
my chest, and my arms.
Finally my teeth began to ache
and my stomach couldn't welcome food.
I hurt.
My whole body hurt
from the tension of trying
and trying
and trying.
My body knew
it couldn't be done.

Memory Song

An old song takes me back.
        I remember all the moments—
the happiness,
the fun of being together.
I am again
young in our relationship.
I miss those days.
I can't have them back,
but I miss them.

If Only . . .

*I*f only..."
How often we look back
on events of life
and speculate, "If only. . . ."
I've done it
with our relationship.
It doesn't really help.
Things can't be redone
even if we had a second chance.
"If only" keeps my gaze
behind me
rather than looking ahead.
Speculation can't replace action.
"If only. . ." never works.

Covenant

We promised
a covenant
in church
for better, worse
richer, poorer
sickness, health
until death.
We broke the promise.
Yet being together
was death
for both of us.
We were no longer healthy.
Today we have another chance
to live again.
Still, it's hard
to break a promise.

Children

In the stresses of separation,
  I sometimes overlook the best—
my children.
They are the product of our dreams
and the promise that things can be better.
They love me
and we can stay together—
growing,
changing,
telling the truth,
and having popcorn on Friday night.
Even though I'm sometimes tired,
weary of responsibility and change,
I have the living gift of children.
Bless them
and bless our life together.

For the Children's Sake

Our children accept us as
            Mom, Dad,
without much qualification.
They only want to feel secure—
loved by both
rather than forced
to choose
or support
a particular parent's
point of view.
It is immensely unfair
to ask them to judge a parent
using a mate's adult standards.
Let children love
both of the people who created them.
For the children's sake
we will not blame
or ask them to reject a parent.
We are adults;
we can cooperate
for the children's sake.

Assurances

You'll never get a divorce,
        will you?"
my son asked when he was nine.
No, I assured him—
but I wasn't sure.
I prayed
that it would never happen.
But it did.
He was sad and frightened,
suggesting that he and his brother
move out for a while
so that we could work things out.
He blamed himself!
I told him it wasn't his fault.
But then I recalled that once
I also told him it would never happen.
It makes me cry to remember.
We let them down.

Security

My older son, fourteen,
         called me home
whenever I stayed at a friend's
too long.
It was annoying—
I wasn't very late
and I needed time away.
But I went home to be with him.
Now I've learned
that children of divorce
fear the added loss
of their "home" parent
after the other parent moves away.
He needed security—
to know I would stay.
It only lasted for a while,
but however long it might have lasted
I'm glad I went home
to be with him.

Broken Home

Some say my children
   come from a "broken home."
I am sad
and offended.
Our home is warm,
welcoming,
loving.
The decision as parents
to separate
changed our lives,
even disrupted them,
but we are not broken.
We are supported,
held together
by God and each other.
We are still a family
of love.

Noncustodial Parent

*I*t is lonely
leaving the children
and going home
alone.
I am sometimes afraid
they'll forget me,
lose interest,
resent my absence,
blame me.
I wonder if there's something
I should be doing for them.
When we're together
it's hard to act naturally.
It takes a while to begin to talk.
This is an awkward time.
Perhaps it's best
to talk candidly about it
with the children.
If each one can say the truth
we can feel closer
and begin to go on.
We'll often be separated
but inwardly united
because our shared emotions
bind us together.

Money

The fact is,
  there's less money now.
Everyone lives with less
and wonders more.
It is an added irritation
to an otherwise perplexing time.
Blame and greed set in
and I find myself
envying not only you
but friends and strangers
who are not so troubled.
It is no wonder
Jesus spoke so often about money.
We are accustomed to having
what we want
and now we must temper
even our wishes
for what we want.
I turn to friends
to get perspective,
to the gospel of Luke,
and to God.

Friends

*F*riends don't know what do to
        or say
when they love two people
who separate.
Like children,
they loathe choosing
and hesitate to say too much
for fear of misunderstanding.
Is loving one
betraying the other?
Can both remain
in the circle of friends?
I have been glad
for those who tell the truth
of their pain
and indecision.
Gradually it all smoothes out
and we rework our relationships,
sustained through hard times
by honest caring.

Phone Calls

*I*n the midst of bedlam
   or silence
the phone rings
and someone wonders,
"Are you all right?"
This precious connection
restores my sense of self
and brushes aside the toil of thoughts
which were churning inside me.
Someone called.
Someone cared.
I'm not alone.

Familiarity

I don't want to go back
or start over
because I don't believe in us anymore.
I am glad for changes,
a sense of self I had lost
and have regained.
Still, there were familiar sounds—
dishes clattering,
the radio station,
and familiar sights—
a cluttered desk,
freshly mown grass,
and a familiar comfortable feeling
that the house was not empty
when I came in the door.
Now and then I miss the familiar.

Small Things

*I*t is the small things that slow me down.
Who shall I send a birthday card to this
year?
A Christmas gift?
How do we talk about those things—
brother-in-law,
mother-in-law,
cousin Sarah whom I love,
and all the relatives I've barely known.
I act out of my heart,
sharing gifts and messages
with those I've known and cared for.
Still, the moments come
when it's hard to decide, to choose.
Is "starting over"
signaled by distance,
or is the continuity of life
cherished in ongoing sharing?
Small things have a way of becoming large.

Anger

I am sometimes amazed at my anger!
Whatever has gone before,
I am surprised to find so much residue
of hostility and anger now.
It is a sign of the investment I've made
in your behavior and welfare
and how it is so entangled with mine.
I am glad for friends who hear me out
and for one who gave me that pillow to hit.
I remember with relief the anger
of Jesus
and David
and Moses.
I can try to pretend it isn't in me,
but it comes seeping out
one way or another.
Let it go!
Don't injure,
don't deny.
Separation and divorce are full of anger.

Justice

Sometimes things seem terribly unfair.
    How does one divide up
love and memories
and balance the scale
with new happenings
and good fortune?
Sometimes one person seems free
to live a new life
while the other is left behind
struggling.
We beat against the impenetrable foe—
injustice—
as if our anger can change it.
Some things cannot change.
Others require more than anger—
they require patience
and careful thought,
confrontation
and time.
Our justice is meager,
our need is for God.

Uncoupling

When we were two
we went about together—
parties,
dinner at friends,
coffee with neighbors.
Now that I'm one
I wonder:
Are the parties still happening?
The dinners, have they stopped?
I set myself to inviting folks in—
couples,
singles,
old friends, new.
People forget, when we aren't two,
that you and I are still whole.
We have interests and talents
and enjoy laughing among friends
just as we used to—
except, not as a couple anymore.
This is a coupled society:
two, four, six, eight.
It's hard to be three, five, or seven.

Another Person

*I*t doesn't make sense
  that I should care
when you are dating someone else.
Our decision is firm
and I would not return.
Yet I feel possessive
and in honest moments
I feel hurt as well.
This is one of those complications
of never being able to neatly segment
life relationships.
It happens when children marry
or friends go away;
a mixture of anger and regret,
with an edge of love,
like ink running on wet paper,
fingering its way across the page.
We do not separate ourselves from love
as neatly as we might wish we could.

Dependency

We used to go to parties—
        crowds of people
standing around talking,
laughing.
Whenever I got bored
or irritated
or tired
I could just ease myself
across the room
to stand beside you.
I didn't have to say a word,
I could just stand there
because we belonged together—
a unit.
Now I am alone.
I have to make the effort
to leave the boredom
or change the conversation
to meet the new people
or speak to the hostess about leaving.
I can't depend on someone else
to be my social avenue.
I've met a lot of interesting people.
Independence helps me grow!

Single

I can tell by the way they say
    single
that people feel sorry for me.
Some of them promise,
"You'll find someone again."
Others tease:
"Have you met any nice person yet?"
There is implicit in their words
the idea that marriage is better
and single is "less than."
It makes me wonder
how always-single people feel
in a coupled society.
I wonder how much the expectations
of people having to be married
influenced my decision to marry
and confused my thoughts of divorce.
I am still a whole person.
I still like basketball
and reading
and snow and dinners out
and children, sunshine, and my work!
I am not less than!

I am me.
Single is not inadequate,
it is like all of life—
bittersweet and good and rich
and full of God,
sadness and promise and fear.
People need not feel sorry for me.

Change

I'm sick of change!
New ways of managing money—
of repairing machines,
washing clothes,
eating dinners.
New experiences meeting people—
entering places alone,
looking for someone to talk to,
wondering what happened to old friends.
New view of myself—
how I've been insensitive,
discovering untapped talents,
thinking of myself as single,
surprising myself with emotions.
Life is so unfamiliar at times,
and I get tired of adjusting,
readjusting,
thinking about myself and my life.
I long for familiar routine.
Change is exhausting
yet exhilarating.
I pause to wonder,
Who would I have been without this change?
I'm tired,
but it's worth the discovery!

Misunderstanding

I feel misunderstood
and it is so frustrating,
so sad!
We share fewer words than ever
and at times they are inadequate
or loaded with personal feelings
which the other cannot know
or has not shared.
We try to be exact
but brief
and we end up feeling hurt
and misunderstood.
This is a painful time
of half-connectedness.
The fabric doesn't tear in a straight line
but has ragged edges
bleeding with frustrations
at not being understood
and having so few ways to retrace,
repeat,
or try to explain.
We are both hurt—
suspended in our inability
to say clearly what we mean.

Uncaring

*A*t times I deride myself
    for being unkind to you.
We have somehow confused
our relationship so much
that we cannot help but hurt,
despite our good intentions.
It is better
just to stay apart.
After years of struggling,
combined with the unspoken ways
we understand each other,
we know what words
or actions
will be hardest for the other
to endure.
I don't even want to do it,
yet I do.
I strike out
and say things
I might once have left inside.
I hurt you
in a way that is unfair.
I am ashamed
and need forgiveness.
It is better just to stay apart.

Holidays

We invest a lot in holidays.
Traditions are important
for they give us a sense
of constancy,
predictability,
and beauty.
Now we must adjust to new ways.
It is scary not to know
whether we can enjoy the day
despite the change.
I tell myself that there is
always change,
even in traditions
on holidays.
What we did at Grandma's
we did not do at Dad's.
Change is the only constant
that does not change.
I will open myself to the days and
enjoy them for what they are—
holy,
special remembrances—
and discover what new traditons
we can develop and love.

Roles

*E*ven though they sometimes changed,
our roles were fairly clear.
We each had our "jobs" to do
and our problems to solve.
Even the children knew—
homework to Mom,
dry cleaning to Dad.
Now everything comes to me
and I don't know where to start.
I am frustrated when children
think I should know everything
and you aren't here to help!
Responsibility taunts freedom.
There is no easy way.

Honesty

*P*eople wait for me
to speak of the divorce.
For a long while
I thought it was their judgment
that kept them silent.
Then I realized it was their love
which didn't want to accentuate
my pain.
I spoke first.
Not a constant rehash of the past
or whining about the present,
but an honest statement
of how I felt:
lonely,
excited,
confused,
relieved,
and even, now and then, angry.
When I could be open
they felt more comfortable
asking and talking with me.
Our tentative steps
formed a trail of support
which we could walk together.

Blame

I find it easy to blame you,
especially when we can no longer
talk it through together.
The ambiguity of the decision
and confusion of living apart—
yet having been tied—
urges me to find a formula.
The answer is:
it's your fault.
Even if it *is* your fault
(a simplistic view
defying most realities),
affixing blame does little to help.
Perhaps I shall soon be done
with having to find cause and fault.
When I am stronger, in time,
I will not need to point to weakness
in order to survive.

Denial

Since we had planned so carefully
    and thought so rationally,
cautiously making our decision,
I thought I would not feel much pain.
But there was something about the sunset
and the tiles in the street
and the fragrance of honeysuckle
that hurled me backwards,
to times before all that rationality,
to moments when planning to be apart
had never entered our minds.
It is inevitable.
I will at times feel great pain,
because I am not only a mind and a plan
but a heart and a memory as well.

Never Again

*T*here are times when the feeling rushes
over me:
It will never happen again.
I will never have a chance for love,
the joy of newness,
the comfort of caring,
the contentment of struggle overcome.
I will always be alone
because somehow I am defective.
I am not lovable now.
All my reason doesn't chase away
this discouraged feeling.
My head hangs low and my step slows,
pondering,
Am I lovable?
Will I ever love again?

Rejection

*I*t is triggered at times by music.
 Some days it comes
when I watch another couple—
young
or old—
walking hand in hand
and sharing together.
It stings—
I feel rejected.
I had as much to do with this choice as you.
Yet I cannot help but feel I am less,
inadequate to your needs.
You have left me
and I feel alone and rejected.
Finding someone else to fill the hollow
is a temporary solution.
I must live with and overcome
rejection,
so that I may begin again.

Psalms

The pages open to psalms easily,
  worn by frequent use,
and following, as they do,
the book of Job,
who also longed to understand.
I am revealed in these psalms, these songs.
I lament,
weep,
cry out in anger,
and confront God with my life.
And I worship,
praise,
hope,
believe, and trust.
Wrapped in these ancient words
are all those emotions and thoughts
which pass in and out of my life daily.
I turn to the timeworn wisdom of God
and God's people
to find my solace and hope.

Reunion

We gather together
formerly family,
now disjointed—
because two of us have divorced.
At first it is very awkward.
People still care.
They have known each other,
perhaps for years,
yet they do not know what to say.
Little by little
we test the waters.
Is it possible to be ourselves
without feeling the estrangement
which divorce implies?
Those who surround us
do not want to choose sides.
They love us—
both of us.
As long as they can remain neutral
there is some hope
for maintaining relationships
and growing in love.

It is a hard time for everyone.
If we can patiently
and understandingly
work at this new status
it is possible that we may salvage
love.
It is not easy.

Tangible

We sometimes focus
on extraneous things:
furniture division,
support payments,
the house sale,
legal fees and pensions.
Our intensity
may not be proportionate
to the items and their values.
They may only be
tangible evidence
of all the togetherness
and division
our lives have endured.

Self-recrimination

I argue with myself.
It was my fault.
No, I'm not to blame.
Yes, I am.
I could have done this.
I should have been that.
Maybe I just didn't try
hard enough
long enough.
And I sigh.
I can't relive the past,
nor find a simple route
through a maze of life experiences,
as if there is an easy answer
to what happened to us.
When I'm tired or prone to doubt
I blame myself—
the easy way out.
It is self-recrimination,
self-destruction,
and it keeps me from going on.

Silences

People don't know what to say at times.
Some choose to say nothing at all.
Those are the hardest times,
and I try to overcome them
with honest feelings.
I understand.
They don't want to hurt me
and don't know what to say.
But silence communicates judgment,
isolation,
and "differentness."
Strained talk seems to say,
"We see you differently now.
You aren't like us anymore."
I try to break through the tension
and speak openly about both yesterday
and tomorrow.
I hope they will risk honesty too.
It's hard to talk alone.

Self-sufficient

I find myself reluctant
to ask other people for help:
a counselor,
a sounding board,
a hug on Sunday morning,
a voice on a quiet night.
Sometimes it is because I'm afraid,
afraid to need people
and afraid to lose someone again.
I lift my chin,
I argue with myself that I should stand alone.
I keep going—
another day,
another week.
It'll get better eventually.
Then, one late afternoon I know.
I can't do it all alone.
I need someone to stand with me.
My fear has robbed me of love,
the very thing I hope most to recover
as I travel this changing road.
Reach out, I tell myself.
Tell someone what you need.
We aren't created to stand alone.

Depressed

*I*t comes on slowly,
        like a shadow across a wall
in the afternoon.
I begin to think I cannot change.
I refuse invitations from friends.
I look for the bleak
and remember cloudy days.
I regret
or resist
or delay making decisions.
Finally a friend says the word—
depressed—
and I realize,
as my eyes sting with tears,
it's true.
I must force myself to fight it.
First I ask, *Am I angry?*
At who?
Say it!
Then I look for things to do.
Say yes to friends
and go for a brisk walk.

Little by little I sense change.
There are more sunny days,
my anger is spoken,
my fear is shared and it collapses.
Depression is difficult
but not impossible.
With help I will change.

Freedom

*F*reedom is not everything we wish,
     but it feels good.
I need this time to discover
what I like,
who I am,
how I've changed,
and where I might like to go.
Choosing for myself
what I want to do for a vacation
or whether I will stay home tonight
is surprisingly interesting
when I have only myself to consult.
I didn't realize
how much I enjoyed music
until I didn't have to wonder
whether you'd like the concert or not.
It's been so long
since I cooked my favorite fish,
I'd forgotten how delicious it tastes.
Freedom isn't everything we dream it will be,
but it feels good.

Dating

The prospect of dating
seems so unfamiliar.
I haven't dated for years.
I'm tossed between
adulthood
and junior high,
and I'm afraid to lose control.
I worry about appearances
and fuss over conversation.
I sometimes "fall in love"
as if I were 17.
I scold myself that I should
know better,
labeling "learning" as a "mistake."
Slowly,
slowly, I say.
Be patient with yourself.
You don't have to take charge.
Just give yourself time
to grow into new life.
You don't have to know everything
all at once.
Be good to yourself and take time.

Vulnerable

*I*t's scary to feel so vulnerable.
 I'm afraid I will not be wise.
I'll so welcome love again
that I'll be blind to dangers.
I notice how attractive other "singles" are
and how easily my heart is moved
when someone shows attention,
understanding,
and care.
I need the assurance of someone's interest
and the touch of someone's hand on mine.
I don't trust my judgment
and I feel unpredictable
and scared.
Give me wisdom to wait,
to think things through.
I can rejoice in renewed feelings,
but temper my vulnerability with time.

Empathy

*L*ife is active and happy,
   but now and then,
when the air is still before rain,
or I tire of the book I've begun,
I pause to think
you might be lonesome today.
This experience of separating
is not mine alone.
I forget that you, too, can feel.
Your home is empty at times
and your memories are dangling like mine.
I don't dwell on the realization,
but I wish resolution and contentment,
not just for me—
but also for you.

Guilt

I know I was wrong.
 There were things I could have done,
words I should have stifled,
times I might have tried harder.
I carry guilts about our past
and sometimes they sit like a stone
leaning on my peace of mind,
ready to roll across my life,
gouging out the carefully laid sod
with which I'm trying to begin again.
I can manage guilt.
I can ask for forgiveness,
perhaps even from you,
and certainly from others
and from God.
I can look at other relationships
with new eyes,
seeking to change my responses
so that the stone might not roll again
and grass can grow.
New life, new ways.
Without guilt.

Resentment

Whatever the source,
        resentment is
an insidious load to bear.
Sometimes it comes from self-pity
or genuine hurt.
Sometimes it is a feeling of
standing still
while you move ahead in some way.
Sometimes it steals in
when I think about
what might have been.
Resentment keeps tallies—
wins and losses,
net gains and deprivations,
60-40, 80-20,
who has the children most,
where's the piano now?
Resentment is self-defeating.
I stand still,
looking backward
or wringing present-day hands.
I must get beyond resentment
if I would begin again.

Confused

I remember taking you to the hospital
and leaving with tears in my eyes,
worried about your coming surgery.
I recall as newlyweds
sudden sweeps of fear,
wondering what I'd do if you were gone,
or were dead.
Now you are gone,
yet living.
Although I can reason the retrospect
of coming to this place,
my emotions are sometimes
confused.
You live, yet we have died,
and there is grief and fear and relief.
Life is not clearly marked.
We are carried in many directions.

Loss

We meet on the street by chance,
once legally related,
now related only by the past
memories,
struggles,
laughter,
and the confidence of trust
that comes with years
of being "family" together.
We laugh again,
talk,
quickly share news,
and promise to have lunch.
Then you are gone
and I sigh.
Loss.
It will never be the same again.

Hurts

For a long time
    I remembered all the hurts:
the unkind words,
the thoughtlessness,
the tears and pain.
It didn't seem to dissipate,
but hung like fog—
even over sunny days.
It would creep up on me
and I would be enveloped
in past miseries.
Lately I've been better.
I've thought about the past,
talked about it,
and prayed about it
until it began to lift.
The fog evaporates faster now
and I'm able to dismiss the past:
I won't think about that.
I want to have a good day.
It is grace which helps us forget
and go on to better thoughts
so that we are not bound to hurts.

Coping

I've always been quite capable,
 trying new things,
reasoning my way through life
with relative success.
This has been a shock.
I can't reason my way
through a dismantled relationship.
Sometimes I don't understand
what caused everything to fall apart.
I can't seem to cope
in my usual ways:
working hard,
persisting,
thinking it through,
persuading.
I'm left on an open plain
where I must walk for miles
before I'll see any rise
or trees or home.
I must find new ways of looking
at life
and myself.
God is at work in this somehow.
Help me find my way!

Touch

Sometimes people do not realize
how important it is
to have a hug.
I don't need passion—
certainly not every day.
But a hug or a knowing handclasp,
even a kind word
spoken with tenderness,
warms me and leaves me
feeling whole again.
We are like babies, really.
Babies need swaddling blankets
wrapped firmly around them
to feel secure,
as they felt before birth.
We need holding—
hugs,
the security of love,
in order to have new birth.
Thank God for people who touch
in love.

Loneliness

Sometimes I am lonely.
     It can happen on Sunday afternoon,
Saturday night,
or even in the middle of a crowd.
What matters is what I do.
It is not always necessary
to run away from loneliness:
busy, busy,
meet the gang,
go to a movie,
call a friend.
Sometimes I just wait a while
and it passes.
Loneliness is part of any life.
Other times it is important
to move out of my lethargy
and find company.
Self-pity is useless and tiring
and there are people
waiting for my phone call
or a letter
or a visit for an hour.

Loneliness is not an enemy
but a moment to be lived.
I have discovered myself
as I meet loneliness
and use it to learn about life.

Taking Risks

As much as I dream of companionship,
new love,
and another chance,
I find myself reluctant—
afraid to take a risk.
Every relationship
feels threatening,
as if it will end in marriage—
and then divorce.
I'm afraid to get hurt.
I regulate my feelings,
only to have them
overcome me suddenly
after being confined so long.
Somehow I must
risk a relationship,
trying new ideas,
new behaviors.
I may get hurt from time to time,
but I'll survive,
and at least I'll know
I'm alive!

Living Alone

*T*he fear of living alone
is not feminine or masculine,
for it invades all our hearts
from time to time:
fear of the dark,
of silence,
of decisions alone;
fear of abandonment,
of inadequacy,
of thieves.
Living alone
is not impossible,
nor is it always unpleasant.
But it is different,
and so we face the unknown
and are afraid.

New Year's Eve

*E*very couple has some special time:
an anniversary,
birthdays,
some memorable date.
Ours was New Year's Eve.
I didn't realize it then.
I do now.
New Year's Eve—
at home as a couple,
at a party,
with friends—
is a good time.
I remember that in later years
of our marriage
I would ponder the night
and hope the next year might be
warmer,
closer,
and intimate.
I had hope on that night
that our relationship might change,
grow,
and rekindle love.
It never did.
Still, it is on New Year's Eve

that I find myself wishing
that I could have a companion.
It seems to be a time
for being together
with someone we love.
The music is nostalgic
and the dream is awakened
that someday I might love again.

Journal Entries

At times I forget
what it was about living together
which drove us apart.
I wonder, not with regret,
but with mystery.
Then I look back—
my journal records it all.
The gradual but insistent eroding
of our nurturing,
our sharing.
There were events,
but mostly feelings
and questions,
a mysterious changing
as we grew distant.
I'm struck by how different we are
from what we'd hoped to be.
I remember now,
and again I understand.

Rejected

She held out her arms to me
        and moved to embrace,
weeping and saying,
"I feel so rejected,
so ugly,
unwanted.
Why does he love someone else?
What have I done
or not done?
Why can't he stay?"
Her tears turned to sobs
and mingled with mine
as I tried to comfort
this grieving woman,
disappointed and afraid.
It was only the start
of months of pain
and self-doubt and anger.
Stay, Lord, stay.
It does not matter why.
Help them see this through.

Betrayal

*U*nhappy in their relationship,
    one sought consolation elsewhere.
It can be devastating
to discover oneself
in love with another while married.
It sours our self-image
and destroys another's trust.
Guilt and shame
distort our days and thoughts
and twist our hearts
in the quiet nights.
This is more than passing interest
or country music lyrics,
for it is betrayal
wrapped in fear.
Turning desire to action
left them standing in the cold,
winter children
in a storm.
Everyone involved was stung
by the winds of regret
and anger and change.
It was devastating.

Admission

At some moment we must say
it was failure.
We were not able
to care enough,
to understand adequately.
I have said and done things
which hurt you
or did not try to help.
I have ignored
or raged
or kept my feelings to myself.
We did not do our best.
It is not a sign
that we should go on together.
It is simply an acknowledgment
that we have sinned.

Forgiveness

*F*orgiveness seems elusive.
   Is it true, God,
that you can forgive me
for this part of my life?
I try to argue that all's well,
that there is nothing to forgive.
Yet at times I cringe,
aware of your intent for our lives
and how we haven't fulfilled it.
Help me not to argue and deny
but accept my lack honestly.
I can say I'm sorry to you.
You always forgive.
I repeat to myself,
God always forgives—
always forgives,
always.

Church

*I*f I never knew before,
    I understand church now.
Church is the group of people
standing together at coffee,
smiling and welcoming me.
Church is a cluster of friends—
separated,
divorced,
widowed—
who talk about how we really feel.
Church is Tom and Diane
saving me a seat beside them in the pew
so that I don't always sit alone.
Church is the community
shaped by the love of Jesus
which embraces all of us
without labels
or questions,
innuendos
or fear.
Bless the church
where I am at home,
even alone.

A Neighbor

Christmas.
 A friend stopped by with a gift.
It wasn't packaged specially.
It was just a message.
"I give to you four hours
of my time
to teach you how to repair
anything you need to fix."
A wonderful, thoughtful gift!
Washing machine, garage door,
stalled car, clogged drain.
We've done them all—
and I learned how.
What is more precious
than time from a friend
and neighbor?
A Christmas gift for all year.

Don't Forget

I remind myself,
don't forget
when you say your prayers
the friends who called
to invite me for dinner,
to offer a ride,
to see how I was,
just to say hi.
These good people
reminded me:
"You'll make it."
"You're doing fine."
"We'll always care."
"You're welcome here."
Say a prayer for each and all
who cared enough to give a call.

Finding a Way

*J*esus told us
  it is not God's intention
that we should divorce.
It is God's wish that we be one—
in marriages,
internationally,
in families,
in friendships,
even within ourselves—
whole, one, and integrated.
God wants our happiness.
But we have not been able
to fulfill God's wish.
We have lived lives of
strife,
misunderstanding,
war, pain,
and divorce.
We have failed.
Jesus told us God's intention.
But Jesus came

because we fail.
We divorce
and turn for forgiveness
and new life
to the one who can help us
and bring us back to God.

Letting Go

I think it was a week,
maybe more,
since I last thought of you.
I haven't tried to forget,
though I was so weary
of always remembering.
It is just that I've begun to change
and I have so much else
to think about.
This is an important realization.
I am no longer so bound
to our past,
our frustrations,
the desire to change you,
and the disappointment.
I have begun to live anew.
I am relieved
and encouraged.
Hope has taken new life
in me.

Someone New

Meeting someone new,
finding a person who gives me
a ray of hope—
not so much for
happily ever after,
but one who is glad for
companionship,
laughter,
and even quiet times—
meeting someone new
is encouraging.
I needed to know
someone might want to be with me
and even begin to care for me.
I don't need to know
that this relationship has a "future."
I only need to enjoy
being happy with someone again.

Alone at the Movies

I'd never gone to a movie alone.
    It seemed a lonely thing to do.
Everyone else was with a friend.
The evenings came
when I wanted to see films,
with or without a companion.
I enjoyed them!
I laughed and cried.
My feelings were as touched
as when I went with others.
I thought about the plot,
the characters,
the scenes.
It was not lonely,
only different.
I discovered independence
and myself
in dialog with me.

Joy

I had no idea that
I could have such fun.
Life has been such effort
for so long
that I'd forgotten how to laugh
or play.
The other day
I acted downright foolishly
and I loved it so!
Look at me, world!
I'm a person
and I'm happy once again!
Thanks, God!

Patience

Someone reminded me
that things take time.
Emotions must be felt and let go.
People must adjust.
But we don't adapt overnight.
Each new experience,
each change
takes its own toll of energy
and patience
and gradual understanding.
Two years, one person said.
I scoffed inside.
As two years pass by
I realize the wisdom of experience.
Things take time to heal.